T0158892

THREE LITTLE WORDS

DANIELLE HEYTHALER

BALBOA.
PRESS

A DIVISION OF HAY HOUSE

Balboa Press books may be ordered through booksellers or by contacting:

Balboa Press
A Division of Hay House
1663 Liberty Drive
Bloomington, IN 47403
www.balboapress.com
1 (877) 407-4847

Print information available on the last page.

ISBN: 978-1-5043-7424-8 (sc)
ISBN: 978-1-5043-7425-5 (hc)
ISBN: 978-1-5043-7452-1 (e)

Library of Congress Control Number: 2017901845

Balboa Press rev. date: 02/07/2017

DEDICATION

A deep, sincere, and heartfelt word of appreciation and gratitude go to Elisha Khurana, Crystal Castle, and Heather Garner for their support, direction, nudges—gentle and firm when I really needed them—and total belief in me.

This book is dedicated to all of you and to my two wonderful daughters, Ashleigh and Bethany. You are a part of the reason this book was created.

INTRODUCTION

So many people go through the motions of daily life without thought or purpose.

They just live without taking the time to think about how they affect others' lives, present themselves to and around others, and think of themselves.

That is the purpose of this book. Dedicating just five to ten minutes of your time to contemplate how just three little words can change everything.

Okay, so what do three little words have to do with you, and why are you even reading this?

Great questions!

It has everything to do with not only you, but also with those who surround you. I am confident you are picking up this book because you care about yourself, your personal growth, and the community with which you interact. You are the type of individual who desires to think deeply about yourself, the world around you, and how you interact with this incredible place and the people you see, maybe only once or every day.

This is not a compilation of cute words to memorize or learn the definitions of or even test your knowledge of, but they are here as more of a personal challenge. It serves as a challenge to you and how you see yourself and the world and how you present yourself to the world in which you live.

Do you want to have better relationships? Of course you do! *Three Little Words* can generate that result.

When you see yourself clearly and want to change, you will take action, and then you and those relationships—public and private—will improve and grow.

Now, if you do not know the definitions of the words contained here, then it would be in your best interest to do a little research. By doing this you will gain so much more from this book, and your life will grow immensely.

I wrote this book to incite a bit of curiosity and self-reflection about the words and phrases included in the book. This is not a 365-day format, as there are not 365 entries.

You are free to review a specific day's entry more than once, view multiple days at the same time, or skip to another page. It would certainly behoove you to examine and incorporate *all* the words and pages in this book

With that said, let's go ahead and move on to the core of this book and the words that will challenge and motivate you and change how you live.

Three Little Words has two sections to ruminate on: Three Separate Words, which contains individual but similar words, and Three-Word phrases, which includes phrases we use regularly.

I wholeheartedly encourage you to skip around the different sections once in a while to break up your time and what you are thinking.

Enjoy, and think deeply!

SECTION I

THREE SEPARATE WORDS

Individual but Similar Words

Each specific set of words is intended to get you to think about yourself. These words are supposed to help you be mindful of your interaction with others and how you perceive yourself.

Do these words apply to me personally?

Do these words apply to me professionally?

Do they apply to what I do?

How do they apply to my behavior toward myself and others privately or publicly?

These are some of the things to consider when going through this section. So let's get started.

1. Thought-provoking

2. Provocative

3. Innovative

1. Borders

2. Boundaries

3. Guidelines

1. Ecstatic

2. Enthusiastic

3. Excited

1. Unstoppable

2. Unbreakable

3. Impervious

1. Peaceful

2. Calm

3. Tranquil

1. Motivated

2. Energized

3. Driven

1. Approachable

2. Accessible

3. Friendly

1. Uplifting

2. Encouraging

3. Supportive

1. Caring

2. Compassionate

3. Loving

1. Mindful

2. Thoughtful

3. Sensitive

1. Trapped

2. Confined

3. Restrained

1. Open

2. Flowing

3. Unrestricted

1. Grounded

2. Rooted

3. Solid

1. Moved

2. Stirred

3. Touched

1. Happy

2. Joyful

3. Bubbly

1. Inspired

2. Challenged

3. Motivated

1. Morose

2. Forlorn

3. Sad

1. Upset

2. Disgusted

3. Reviled

1. Circumnavigating

2. Circumambulating

3. Mobile

1. Chilled

2. Frosty

3. Cold

1. Vowed

2. Promised

3. Assured

1. Alive

2. Rejuvenated

3. Lively

1. Wowed

2. Amazed

3. Fascinated

1. Fortitude

2. Strength

3. Power

1. Outspoken

2. Bold

3. Unhindered

1. Quiet

2. Shy

3. Reserved

1. Funny

2. Silly

3. Goofy

1. Charmed

2. Blessed

3. Fortunate

1. Magnificent

2. Marvelous

3. Fantastic

1. Obvious

2. Clear

3. Transparent

1. Focused

2. Concentrated

3. Single-minded

1. Annoyed

2. Aggravated

3. Irritated

1. Rigorous

2. Tough

3. Demanding

1. Obstacle

2. Hindrance

3. Hurdle

1. Tortured

2. Tormented

3. Punished

1. Ruminate

2. Contemplate

3. Consider

1. Mesmerizing

2. Captivating

3. Enchanting

1. Embellished

2. Enhanced

3. Supplemented

1. Babied

2. Coddled

3. Cradled

1. Longing

2. Desiring

3. Craving

1. Rules

2. Laws

3. Dictates

1. Suppressed

2. Captive

3. Enslaved

1. Habitual

2. Perpetual

3. Constant

1. Tremble

2. Shake

3. Quiver

1. Boisterous

2. Loud

3. Obnoxious

1. Sage

2. Insightful

3. Wise

1. Spry

2. Feisty

3. Energetic

1. Cheerful

2. Optimistic

3. Joyous

1. Reiterate

2. Repeat

3. Copy

1. Original

2. Fresh

3. New

1. Amenable

2. Agreeable

3. Unopposed

1. Aplomb

2. Self-confidence

3. Assurance

1. Rudimentary

2. Basic

3. Fundamental

1. Collide

2. Clash

3. Conflicting

1. Slovenly

2. Messy

3. Untidy

1. Impenetrable

2. Invulnerable

3. Invincible

1. Engaged

2. Connected

3. Intertwined

1. Covenant

2. Pact

3. Contract

1. Unruly

2. Rebellious

3. Lawless

1. Unfettered

2. Liberated

3. Free

1. Abhorrent

2. Abnormal

3. Unusual

1. Hesitant

2. Cautious

3. Wary

1. Treacherous

2. Dangerous

3. Unsafe

1. Undependable

2. Unpredictable

3. Unreliable

1. Forced

2. Coerced

3. Pressured

1. Relevant

2. Applicable

3. Pertinent

1. Buddy

2. Pal

3. Friend

1. Valid

2. Viable

3. Useful

1. Revered

2. Respected

3. Honored

1. Wrecked

2. Destroyed

3. Obliterated

1. Broken

2. Shattered

3. Dismantled

1. Late

2. Tardy

3. Unpunctual

1. Dissipated

2. Dissolved

3. Melted

1. Jubilant

2. Rejoicing

3. Celebratory

1. Beautiful

2. Gorgeous

3. Pretty

1. Standards

2. Principles

3. Mandates

1. Intelligent

2. Brilliant

3. Genius

1. Experienced

2. Learned

3. Knowledgeable

1. Distanced

2. Separated

3. Segregated

1. Committed

2. Disciplined

3. Intent

SECTION II

THREE-WORD PHRASES

Phrases We May Use Regularly but Whose Possible
Full Impact We Do Not Always Consider

This specific set of three-word phrases is included to get us to consider the possible impact we and our words have on the lives of others.

So let us begin by being mindful of what we say to others, starting with this short list. This is obviously not an exhaustive list, so if you discover another phrase, please add it to your book.

We are only going to show one phrase per day to minimize any possible confusion or excessive contemplation on these.

Take the time to thoroughly review the phrases, and see how they could change not only the life of another person, but your life too.

Consider how many times we say this, to whom it is said, and how it is said.

Words carry life and the ability to heal, hurt, bless, and support and can have negative impact if used improperly.

I love you!

I am sorry!

Let me help.

On my way!

I was wrong!

You got this!

Time to go!

You were right!

Who am I?

What's your name?

Leave it alone!

(Let it go.)

How are you?

You're doing great!

Here we are!

You look incredible.

Can we talk?

Who are you?

Are you ready?

Where is mine?

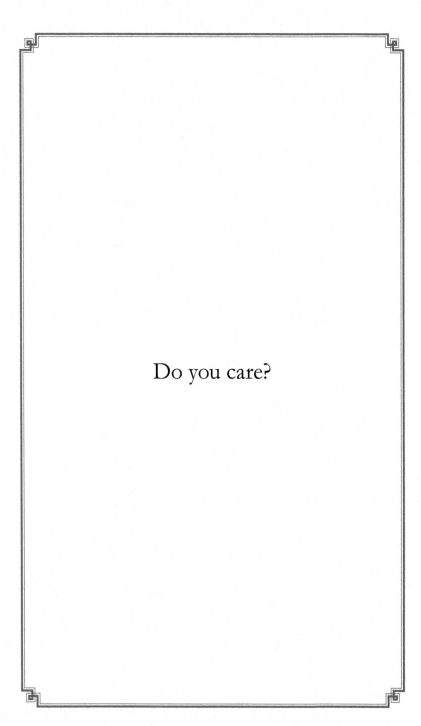

Do you care?

AFTERWORD

Words have power. They have the power to change your life and your world. They can change it in both positive and negative ways. Words can be both simplistic and complex. They can have different meanings based on the context and the intent of how they are spoken or written

This book was formed by the many events where I did or did not think about whom I would have an impact on and how my life would affect them. It was the realization afterward that drove me to seek the needed change of present-moment mindfulness.

Let's be ever mindful of our life and who we share it with, because we will have an effect on everyone we meet whether we want to or not.

How do you want to be known and remembered?